lyrics by
Mark Adamo

music by
John Corigliano

METAMUSIC
three songs for theater voice and piano

ED 4503

First Printing: April 2012

ISBN: 978-1-4584-5673-1

G. SCHIRMER, Inc.

DISTRIBUTED BY

HAL•LEONARD®
CORPORATION

7777 W. BLUEMOUND RD. P.O. BOX 13819 MILWAUKEE, WI 53213

DODECAPHONIA

I had always wanted to write a cabaret song entitled "They Call Me Twelve-Tone Rose," only because the delicious absurdity of the title appealed to me. I made the mistake of mentioning this to Mark Adamo as he was writing the libretto for his opera *Little Women*, and before long the complete lyric appeared on my desk. (Full disclosure demands that I admit to contributing the word "ha!" to the last stanza.) I procrastinated, in my usual way, but then blundered again, this time mentioning to Joan Morris over dinner that the lyric existed. Joan, of course, is not only a bewitching cabaret singer in her own right, but she performs evenings of theatre and cabaret song all over the world with her husband, the internationally recognized composer William Bolcom, at the piano. Finally, after Joan's postcard reading, "Are you going to make a diva beg?" I composed (in strict dodecaphonic manner) the brief film-noir aria before you.

—JC

Dodecaphonia was first performed on May 22, 1997,
by Joan Morris, mezzo-soprano and William Bolcom, piano;
Symphony Space, New York, NY
It has been recorded by Lisa Delan, soprano, and Kristin Pankonin, piano
And If The Song Be Worth A Smile - Songs by American Composers
(Pentatone B001LKLKWK)

Duration 4 minutes

MARVELOUS INVENTION

...also, indirectly, owes its life to Joan Morris and Bill Bolcom, as it was their tasty performance of "Dodecaphonia" at the Kaplan Penthouse that prompted those sultans of song Steven Blier and Michael Barrett to commission this companion piece, of which Theodora Hanslowe sang the first performance. For a few brief years, when music-players and phones were separate appliances, performances of this piece required substantial prop rehearsal, but the iPhone's changed all that, as it has so many things.

—MA

Marvelous Invention was originally commissioned by the New York Festival of Song
in collaboration with Meet the Composer.
It was first performed on March 22, 2001 by Theodora Hanslowe
at the Kaye Playhouse, New York, NY.
It has been recorded by Lisa Delan, soprano, and Kristin Pankonin, piano
And If The Song Be Worth A Smile - Songs by American Composers
(Pentatone B001LKLKWK)

Duration 5 minutes

End of the Line

This is certainly the most personal of the three lyrics to me, as I'm old enough to remember 78s and hi-fi. (On the other hand, as I've mentioned elsewhere, it was the [then] high-technology recording of Copland's *Billy the Kid* that first made me want to be a composer to begin with, so I'm not such a technophobe as all that.) This lyric doesn't privilege what's been gained over what's been lost, and so most of the time the music doesn't either: it's only the stuttering timing of the last lines that gives the listener, I hope, a hint of the loneliness pulsing just beneath the narrator's new-toy delight.

—JC

End of the Line was first performed on July 17, 2009,
by Joan Morris, mezzo-soprano and William Bolcom, piano
Mohawk Trail Concerts, Shelburne Falls, MA

Duration 4 minutes

They seem like a unified set now, but these songs grew one by one over 12 years. After writing "Marvelous Invention" we had two tart, language-driven comedies about music for moderns: but two songs aren't enough for a set, really, and both of us wanted a third musical subject that would call forth a mellower setting than the first two. When first Patelson's Music Store in the West 50s and then Tower Records disappeared, the topic was unmissable; the lyric to "End of the Line" was written in a single day.

—MA

for more information:

www.johncorigliano.com   www.markadamo.com   www.schirmer.com   www.halleonard.com

DODECAPHONIA

I was a cop on the (off-)beat,
Assigned the strangest case:
Some morbid seductress, some sinister vamp
Was stalking composers of every camp.
I'd very few clues for the chase:

(The pianist plays six unrelated pitches.)

Her coat—a battered ermine,
One victim recollected:
Her accent—faintly German,
Another one suspected.
She'd left no other trace.

(The pianist plays six more pitches, different from the first six.)

I needed to determine
How all this was connected.
I started to pace.

(The pianist plays the twelve tone row as the singer paces, thinking...)

Ermine coat...
German throat...
O, mein Gott!

It hit me so subtly
It was almost subliminal:
That I was pursuing no less than the town's most
Notorious
Serial
Criminal:

They call her Twelve-Tone Rose,
And oh! She's cold.
She sounds completely schizoid, but she's so controlled.
She never quite repeats herself, yet always sounds the same:
That too, too Teutonic, that anti-mnemonic,
That dodecaphonic dame—
Whose name is Twelve-Tone Rose.

Don't buy her line!
Her ev'ry fey *non sequitur* is by design,
She lured the likes of Bernstein, even Copland to her camp,
That sometimes ethereal, always funereal,
Post-Wagnerial vamp.

Sure,
She's exotic as a Persian,
As Beguiling as a witch;
And all your smartest friends take her advice.
But she'll lure you to inversion
And you'll fall for ev'ry pitch,
'Cause she'll never use the same pitch twice.

No, no, beware of Twelve-Tone Rose, (ha!)
She's no good for laughs;
And she'll take your ev'ry melody and leave you with graphs!
She'll take your pride, your heart, your wit, and when she's done
You, too, will be vaguely bathetic, completely synthetic,
And just no fu —

(Pianist stops dramatically in mid-phrase, beckons singer to piano and whispers in his/her ear.)

(Singer speaks...)
What? Another one?
Young . . . American . . . stutters?

They call her
Thoroughly Post-Modern
Millie Millie Millie Millie
Millie Millie Millie Millie
Millie Millie Millie Millie
Millie Millie Millie Millie...

Sorry—gotta run!

MARVELOUS INVENTION

(A well-heeled subscriber, on her phone, toys with the newest, smallest, most fashionable personal music player—which might well be her phone.)

Darling, don't be angry, but that concert? Not tonight.
No, keep the ticket, really: go! Enjoy!
I know: it's so last minute—*please* don't take it as a slight.
It's only that I've purchased the most marvelous new toy.

This small invention (right now it's playing 'Geny Kissin!)
Has wholly revolutionized the way I listen:

I now hear Joshua Bell playing all Ravel over *crème caramel* at Chanterelle,
Or Natalie Dessay* interpreting Messiaen. (Such a feast!)
I love Emanuel Ax playing Arnold Bax as I choose my slacks from the racks at Saks,
Or Barbra Streisand in Floyd's *Of Mice and Men*. (It wasn't released.)
I play my Thomas Ades or C. P. E. Bach during Pilates at the Reebok,
Then out to the street to Purcell's *Suite from Queen Mab*.
I need my hit of Max Roach when in business class:
If I'm stuck in coach, give me Philip Glass,
Die Schöne Müllerin, or Gunther Schuller in the cab.

Why do I need the concert hall?
Why do I need performance at all?
With the tickets and the sitter and the parking and the chatter—it's a drag.
Give me my discs and one fast hour,
And I'll have the classical section of Tower...
     (sighing, wistfully) Tower...
Alphabetized and perfectly sized for even an evening bag.

So play me Sondheim or Takemitsu when it's time to walk my Shih-Tzu,
Or *Ruslan and Ludmilla*, if not the Debussy *La Mer*.
I crave my Malfitano singing Corigliano with Robert Spano on piano
     with my Montepulciano at Da Silvano,
Or a Bolla with Bolcom passeth all compare!

Darling, it's truly a new world order.
Now with my magical disc recorder,
Why on earth would anybody ever want or need to hear their music live?
With my perfectly marvelous invention—
(Here's Sousa, Ned Rorem, the Schoenberg *Brettl-lieder!*)
Its benefits too numerous to mention—
(La Chiusa, and *Forum*, and Adam Guettel *lieder!*)
Best of all... Best of all, I barely need to pay attention...

(She reconsiders.)

Darling: meet me down at "Will Call" at seven-forty-five.

---

* *The performer has the option of correcting the misplaced accent on "Dessay" or making a comic point of it.*

END OF THE LINE

It first was a record store: corner of Main;
Seventy-eights, to hi-fi.
Music, and music, and music!
In a cluttered, an overstocked aisle.
When the owner was busy, you'd wait:
      With the fan of Chopin,
      With the Ellington man,
      With the show-queen who knew all the tunes from *Can-Can*,
With your neighbors and friends
In line.

It then added video: crowds were insane.
Horror, and porn, and sci-fi.
Movies, T V— but still, music!
In an aisle the breadth of a mile.
When the cashiers were busy, you'd wait:
      With the guy on his phone
      Justifying Stallone,
      With the punk on her Walkman, in some private zone,
And the rest of the mob
In line.

      Some how, improbably, on it went:
      Stubbornly persevered.
      But prices kept rocketing, and so did the rent.
      And little by little the neighbors,
      And the need,
      Disappeared.

So now it's a coffee bar: part of a chain.
Soy milk, green tea, free Wi-Fi.
To download a cosmos of music,
You have only to click on a file.
When the server is busy, you wait:
      Only you and your screen,
      Solitary, serene,
      Those other consumers unheard and unseen...
A pseudonymous guest of your faraway hosts,
You sip and you wait,
      With the rest of the ghosts...
Online.

to Joan Morris and Bill Bolcom
METAMUSIC
1. DODECAPHONIA

Mark Adamo

John Corigliano

I was a cop on the (off)-beat, __ As-signed the strang-est case: Some mor-bid se-duc-tress, some sin-is-ter vamp, Was stalk-ing com-pos-ers of ev-'ry camp. I'd ver-y few clues for the chase: Her

(she/he cocks her/his head at the high "G" and counts pitches)

coat— a bat-tered er-mine, One vic-tim re-col-lect-ed; Her

ac-cent— faint-ly Ger-man, An-oth-er one sus-pect-ed. She'd

left no oth-er trace. I need-ed to de-

ter-mine How all this was con-nect-ed. I start-ed to

2. MARVELOUS INVENTION

♩ = ca. 80

(The Singer—an urbane woman in a comfortable tax bracket–speaks into her phone.)

Darl-ing, ___ don't be an - gry, ___ but that con-cert? Not to-night.

No, keep the tick-et, real-ly: go! ___ En - joy! I know– it's so last-min-ute– *please* don't

(She produces the newest, smallest, most powerful music player, and dons the earphones.)

take it as a slight. It's on - ly that I've pur-chased the most mar-vel-ous new toy. ___

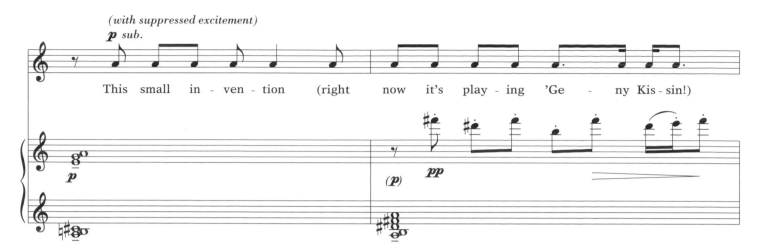

(with suppressed excitement)

This small in-ven-tion (right now it's play-ing 'Ge-ny Kis-sin!)

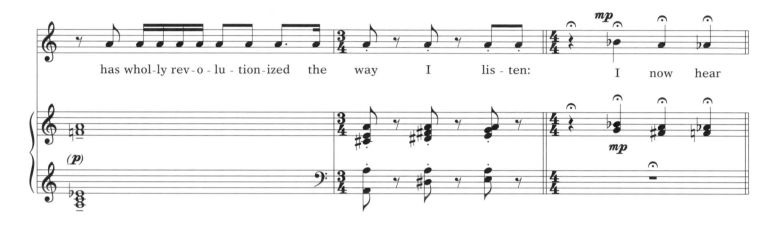

has whol-ly rev-o-lu-tion-ized the way I lis-ten: I now hear

Easy (♩ = 80)

Josh-u-a Bell play-ing all Rav-el___ ov-er crème car-a-mel at

Chant-er-elle, ___ Or Na-ta-lie Des-say___ in-ter-pret-ing Mes-sia-en. ___

(Such a feast!) I love E - man-u - el Ax__ play - ing

Ar - nold Bax__ as I choose my slacks from the racks at__ Saks,__ Or Bar - bra Strei-sand in

Floyd's *Of Mice and Men.* (It was-n't re-leased.) I play my Tho - mas A - dès__ or

C. P. E. Bach dur-ing Pi - la - tes at the Ree - bok, Then out to the street__ to

Pur - cell's_ Suite_ from Queen Mab._____ I need my hit of Max Roach_ when _ in

busi - ness _ class:_ if I'm stuck in _ coach,_ give me Phi - lip _ Glass, _____ Die

schö - ne Mül-ler-in,_ or Gun - ther Schul-ler in___ the cab.

Why do I need the con-cert hall? Why do I need per-form-ance at all? With the

tick-ets and the sit-ter and the park-ing and the chat-ter it's a drag.

Give me my discs and one fast hour, and I'll have the clas-si-cal sec-tion of Tower...

*: Cue sized notes may be sung *ossia.*

ad lib.　　　　　in time

(mp) sighing, wistfully　p

To - wer... Al - pha - bet - ized_ and per - fect - ly sized for ev - en an eve - ning bag.

So play me Sond - heim_ or Ta - ke - mit - su __ when it's

time to walk my Shih - Tzu, _ Or Rus - lan and Lud - mil - la, __ if

(humming)

not the De - bus - sy La __ Mer. __ Mmm _____

Its ben-e-fits___ too nu-mer-ous to men-tion,

(shouted)
(La Chi-usa, and *For-um,* and Ad-am Guet-tel lied-er) ___ Best of all... ___ Best of all, ___

rall.
(change to speech)   *(She thinks a moment and takes off her earphones.)*   *(brightly)*

___ I bare-ly need to pay... at-ten-tion...   Darling,

Allegro ♩ = 144
(She hangs up.)

Meet me down at "Will Call"
at seven-forty-five.

*: The C♯ may be omitted.

3. END OF THE LINE

♪ = ca. 96

It first was a re-cord store: cor-ner of Main;

Se-ven-ty-eights___ to hi-fi. Mu-sic, and mu-sic, and mu - sic!___ In a

clut-tered, an o-ver-stocked aisle. When the ow - ner was bu - sy,

you'd wait:___ With the fan___ of Cho - pin, With the El - ling-ton man, With the

show-queen who knew all the tunes from "Can - Can," With your neigh-bors and

friends In line. It then ad-ded vi-de- o: crowds were in-sane.

Hor- ror, and porn,___ and sci - fi.___ Mo- vies, T V—but still, Mu - sic!___ In an

aisle___ the breadth of a mile. When the ca-shiers were bu - sy,

neigh-bors, And the need,_____ Dis - ap - peared._____

rall. **Tempo 1 (♪ = ca. 96)**

So now it's a cof-fee bar: part of a chain.

(p)

Soy milk, green tea,___ free Wi - Fi. To down - load a cos - mos of

(p)

mu - sic,___ You have on-ly to click on a file. When the

mp ———— *p*

(Slower)

(p)

ser - ver is bu - sy, You wait:___ On - ly you and your screen, So - li -

pp *' ppp*

ta - ry, se - rene, Those o - ther con - su - mers un - heard and un - seen... A pseu -

rall. **Tempo I**

(♪ = ca. 96) *p*

do - ny-mous guest of your far - a - way hosts, You sip and you wait,

ppp *p*

poco rall al fine. *pp*

with the rest of the ghosts... On - line.

pp